THE Wine and WORD

SAVOR & SERVE

By
Kurt Senske

For more information about Kurt Senske,
and to inquire about his speaking availability on this topic
please visit his website: www.kurtsenske.com

Cover photograph: Nathan B. Harrmann.

Interior photographs: Laurie Senske.

Creative Communications for the Parish
1564 Fencorp Dr.
Fenton, MO 63026

1-800-325-9414

www.creativecommunications.com

ISBN 978-1-889387-76-5

Printed in the U.S.A.

TABLE OF CONTENTS

PRAISE FOR
WINE AND THE WORD

Passion for a rich life in Christ, the Vine, flows from every page of Senske's book. He challenges us to be mature in character as we reflect the work of God in and through the fruit of our lives.

– Cindy Steinbeck, president of Steinbeck Vineyards &
Winery and author of *The Vine Speaks*

Really? When my friend, Dr. Kurt Senske, first shared this book concept with me, I was skeptical. Despite his compelling legacy of transformative Christian leadership—not to mention his oenophilia (love of fine wine)—could he pull off this project? Could he make clear the spiritual link between a fermented beverage and a dynamic, biblical faith? I must concede: after consuming this book, my appreciation for both wine and God's Word has deepened. Senske's work is choice. Taste and see for yourself. Really!

– Rev. John Nunes, Jochum Chair professor,
Valparaiso University

CHAPTER 1
The Nectar of the Gods

If God forbade drinking, would he have made wine so good?

Cardinal Richelieu

Famed theologian Paul Tillich accurately describes wine as both divine and human and truly the "nectar of gods."[1] He reminds us that wine (or grape juice, its unfermented cousin)—being the only beverage used as a sacramental drink—is a gift from God. He provides the proper soil conditions, temperature, sunshine and rain for a successful harvest. And God calls us to serve as *vignerons*—

servants of the soil—to decide which variety of grape to plant, tend the vines, pick the harvest and then carefully determine where and how long to age the wine. The fermenting process itself, however, is God's alone, and continues long after the grape-become-wine finds its home in the bottle. Tillich writes with an almost intimate knowledge of the substance:

First it is a baby, then it is a child, then it enters puberty and becomes a teenager, then it becomes a young adult, then wine reaches its full maturity, and slowly it enters old age—some wines gracefully, some harshly, and then it dies. Of all drinks, wine alone recapitulates life. This is why wine is a sacrament.[2]

Of course, like any alcoholic beverage, wine can have a negative impact on our life and our faith. Abusing it cuts a wide destructive path that can lead to highway fatalities, domestic violence, addiction, broken families and hangovers.

The consequences of excessive drinking, however, are not the focus of this book; the author has a higher expectation of his readers and of himself. I have devoted the past decade of my life to writing and speaking about what it means to live and work as a Christian in the 21st century.[3] This book follows in the same vein; I am writing to fellow believers who weave their appreciation for God's creative handiwork into the fabric of their Christian calling. And I ask you to indulge me in using wine as a metaphor for the Christian life. This is an invitation to join me, and drink, if you will, the exquisite mead of God's Word—perhaps while sipping your favorite beverage at home, in an airplane or wherever life finds you at this moment.

Some would say that wine, at its best, is divine, a honeyed elixir that soothes the spirit, and the drinking of it a sensuous experience. Those of us who love the fruit of the vine find ourselves lingering in our favorite wine store, studying the wine list of offerings and eagerly awaiting the next issue of *Wine Spectator*. We might even travel to numerous continents to educate ourselves about oenology, the science of wine. But the pursuit of such knowledge reveals much more—we learn how we relate to ourselves, to each other and to all of God's creation.

Wine engages our senses fully; it is cerebral and sensuous, secular and sacred, historic and modern, seductive and destructive, civilized and edgy. As we travel the wine path, we might be surprised by what awaits us; it is a journey down literary alleyways, through historic districts and across oceans as we grow in appreciation of its artistic subtlety and marvel at its commercial success. Along the way there are thousands of varieties of grapes to taste, a myriad of appellations and quality designations to learn and hundreds of winemaking methods to study—each of which produces its own unique glassful, be it fortified, sparkling, late harvest or ice. Wine has been written about through the ages—by the Old Testament prophets, Mago of Carthage, Virgil, Horace, Cato, Varro, Columella, Martial, Plato, Aristophanes, Baudelaire, Byron, Dickens, Joyce, Tolstoy, Johnson, Robinson, Lynch, Asher—and now, to state the obvious, Senske.

As members of the wine tribe, we sometimes use descriptors that an outsider might consider over-the-top. Non-cult members howl in amusement and disbelief when we notice the scent of a flowery perfume, a whiff of tobacco or a hint of butter following the first sip. For my part, I tend to define my wine experience more by people and place than hints of mocha and charred herb. I clearly recall the carafe of Provence Rosé my wife, Laurie, and I recently shared at a Parisian café on the Rue de Rivoli or the silky Pommard three generations of Senskes enjoyed while sitting in a cave-like bistro in Beaune.

In my Christian walk, I have considered how one might study the Scriptures with the same careful appreciation one gives to the study of wine—we regard the depth of its color, scrutinize the label, smell the cork, pour and swirl the wine in our glass, take several quick, short sniffs to experience its "nose" and savor it in our mouth, letting it linger before swallowing. By drinking deeply of God's wisdom, commands and promises, we taste and see that the Lord is good, that he satisfies our deepest needs and that our reverence for him is indeed the beginning of wisdom. Entering the pages of the Bible is like taking a seat at a never-ending banquet, where the fare is plentiful, but can never be totally consumed. To quote Martin Luther—a lover of both wine and the Word—in his observation about studying the Scriptures, "There is always something left over to understand and to do. Therefore, you must never be proud, as if you were already full."[4]

In our 23 years of marriage, my wife and I have been introduced to experiences that, except for the generosity of friends and colleagues wealthier than we are, we never would have enjoyed. One especially memorable evening in Rome included an 18-course private "business dinner" (more accurately, a decadent, over-the-top food orgy), coupled with pairings of fine Italian wine that included Prosecco, a crisp Frascati, a Super Tuscan, an exquisite Piedmont Barolo, a Chardonnay (from Sicily, of all places) and a little grappa to end the night. In the years of our haphazard wine tutorial, through experiences such as these (the rest being of more moderate proportion), we have slowly come to appreciate the complexity and richness of the subject. While our bank account has taken a modest hit, the nature and quality of our lives has been enriched. Our wine-infused conversations steadily drifted to a more mystical level. Exploration of the art of making a fine wine opened a window into the art of living a meaningful life. We shared with friends and family how lessons from the vineyard have given direction on our quest to live the life God has called us to live.

At first blush, the worlds of wine and Christian living may seem unconnected, even opposed to one another. The one is often associated with frivolity and the hedonistic pleasures of our temporal life, while the other is focused on the cross and the grace that enables our service to others and that grants eternal life. But first impressions can be deceiving. The complexity and artistic challenge of tending the vineyard—the miracle of the cycles of the seasons, the craft of the *vigneron* in fulfilling her God-given vocation, the resultant blessing of the wine's varietal character— all provide us with an opportunity to rediscover and invigorate our own lives. The art and the miracle of wine, coupled with the rich biblical imagery of the vineyard, open a lens onto God's rich and abundant grace, and, in turn, onto our lives as disciples.

I am not a wine expert. My wife and I describe ourselves as enthusiastic, always-learning oenophiles (the French might dismissively label us *amateurs de vin*, or wine amateurs). Nor am I a religious scholar. Through the words I "pen" here, I am hoping to chronicle my life's path as sinner and saint. My prayer is that in reading these pages you might see similarities in your own Christian walk. I hope our journey together—with detours through Napa, Tuscany, Bordeaux, Coonawarra, Burgundy and Rioja—will be a fruitful one. I invite you to pour a glass of your favorite drink (wine, if you are inclined) and join me as we trace how the branches of our lives lead from Christ, the Vine, out into the world.

CHAPTER 2

The Vine and the Bible

Wine is God's special drink. The purpose of good wine is to inspire us to a livelier sense of gratitude to God.

John Calvin

Our journey begins in the Bible, wherein wine is deeply rooted, metaphorically and literally, in the Old and New Testaments. The grapevine is the tree most often cited in the Scriptures (205 times), and references to wine or to the vine number an astonishing 521. During biblical times wine was integral to daily life and was an immediate

and effective symbol to which everyone, regardless of social status, could relate.

In the Old Testament wine was regarded as a necessity of life and as part of even the simplest meal (Genesis 14:18). A fortress was stocked with it (2 Chronicles 11:11), and it was consumed by even the very young (Lamentations 2:12; Zechariah 9:17). Wine was considered a staple (Genesis 27:28), and a year without a grape crop, due to weather or destruction by foreigners, was a calamity (Deuteronomy 28:30, 39; Isaiah 62:8; Micah 6:15). An abundant wine harvest was considered a special token of God's blessing

(Genesis 27:28; Deuteronomy 7:13; Amos 9:14) and an extraordinarily good harvest a sign of the Messianic Age (Amos 9:13; Joel 3:18; Zechariah 9:17). Wine was used in a variety of situations. It was a festive drink (Esther 5:6), a disinfectant (Luke 10:34) and a drug (Mark 15:23). It was the medium chosen by Jesus on the occasion of his first miracle (John 2:1-11), and it was—and continues to be—the earthly substance that is his blood in the mystery of the Lord's Supper (Matthew 26:27-29).

The deleterious effects of drinking too much wine are likewise listed (more than 70 references), many of them found in the Book of Proverbs, which notes that it leads to violence (4:17), mockery (20:1), making a man poor (23:20-21), having it bite like a serpent (23:31-32) and impairing judgment (31:4-5). It inflames passion, according to Isaiah 5:11, and enslaves the heart (Hosea 4:11). Like all of God's gifts, wine is meant to be enjoyed in moderation. A "gladdening of the heart" through moderate consumption is looked upon favorably (Esther 1:10; Psalm 104:15; Ecclesiastes 9:7).

The first mention of wine comes in Genesis, after the flood, when "Noah, a man of the soil, proceeded to plant a vineyard" (Genesis 9:20). The verses following detail how he, the first vintner, drank too much of his own harvest, resulting in a very unfortunate family incident. It is an all-too-common example of how we can turn God's miraculous creation into a destructive weapon.

In the Old Testament the Lord directs the people of Israel to include a *hin* of wine, or about two liters, as part of their offering to him: "It will be an offering made by fire, an aroma pleasing to the Lord" (Numbers 15:8-10). Wine was given as a gift. Abraham, returning from victory in battle, is blessed by King Melchizedek, who offered him bread and wine as a sign of hospitality and friendship (Genesis 14:17-19). When King Saul, in a fit of pique, asked that Jesse have his young son David come and play the harp for him, Jesse sent with David a housewarming gift of bread, wine and a young goat (1 Samuel 16:20). And the first toast in the Bible was made by the pagan King Belshazzar at a banquet in 539 B.C. celebrating his father's plundering of the Jewish temple. Picture in your mind the debauchery and decadence of the affair:

> King Belshazzar gave a great banquet for a thousand of his nobles and drank wine with them . . . . [H]e gave orders to bring in the gold

and silver goblets that Nebuchadnezzar his father had taken from the temple in Jerusalem so that the king, his nobles, his wives and his concubines might drink from them . . . . As they drank the wine, they praised the gods of gold and silver, of bronze, iron, wood and stone (Daniel 5:1-4).

In the midst of the celebration, words began appearing on the wall directly behind the inebriated king, who inquired what they meant. Daniel, interpreting the message, charged the king with sinning through disobedience and pride, defying God by desecrating the sacred vessels and praising idols. What began as a joyous occasion, complete with hearty toasts, ended badly for the king, who later that evening was killed by his enemies.

Perhaps the most well-known biblical wine reference takes place at the wedding in Cana. In attendance with Jesus were his mother, Mary, and his disciples. (From this and other references in the Gospels, we can infer that Jesus enjoyed a good time.) The wedding host was obligated to provide a feast that measured up to the standards of the societal pecking order—no small feat, given that these celebrations typically lasted up to a week. The wine flowed freely throughout the fete, and for the host to run out would be a serious faux pas.

What I love about this story is that even though Jesus is Jesus after all, he complies almost immediately with his mother's request—albeit with some holy hesitation. Although fully acquainted with his humanity, Mary likely was unaware of his divine capacity. Nonetheless, she approaches Jesus to spare the host the embarrassment of having no more wine. Mary's interference speaks of her concern for the host (tinged perhaps with a bit of pride in her son). In the process, Jesus turns the water into some of the finest wine. No supermarket swill for him. Ben Franklin mused that the purpose of this miracle was to demonstrate that wine is "a constant proof that God loves us and loves to see us happy."[5]

CHAPTER 3

The Power of Imagery and Symbolism

A bottle of wine contains more philosophy than all the books in the world.

Louis Pasteur

New York Times chief art critic Michael Kimmelman reminds us that "art provides us with clues about how to live our lives more fully . . . . [E]verything, even the most ordinary daily affair, is enriched by the lessons that can be gleaned by art . . . ."[6] The inspired scribes who wrote

the books of the Bible were artists in their own right, employing the vivid imagery of the vineyard as instruction for the entire gamut of life—birth, sickness, health, vocation, romance, hope, despair, death, damnation and resurrection. Wine is used as a symbol of prosperity and blessing. Jacob wishes for his son Judah a prosperous life:

> He will tether his donkey to a vine, his colt to
> the choicest branch; he will wash his garments
> in wine, his robes in the blood of grapes. His
> eyes will be darker than wine, his teeth whiter
> than milk (Genesis 49:11-12).

The vineyard is a vivid symbol of the coming of the Messianic Age:

CHAPTER 4

What Is Your Varietal Character?

t extractive note of an aged cork being
wn has the true sound of a [person] opening
her] heart.

William Benwell

 no two people are exactly alike, so each
 of wine has its own character. There are
ly thousands of types, each presenting itself
ue way. Karen MacNeil, in her informative
 Wine Bible, describes five qualities to assess

In ancient Israel, a goatskin was often the container of choice for wine. As the grape juice fermented, the skin would stretch. A skin already stretched by use would break with the unfermented liquid. Jesus uses this word-picture to illustrate how his presence makes a business-as-usual existence impossible; our old forms cannot contain the radical newness of the Gospel Christ embodies:

> Neither do men pour new wine into old wineskins. If they do, the skins will burst, the wine will run out and the wineskins will be ruined. No, they pour new wine into new wineskins, and both are preserved (Matthew 9:17).

The stomping of grapes with human feet is an ancient tradition. The owners of the vineyard would lighten the winepresser's task by making a festival of the occasion and would hire a piper to play. The tempo of the music encouraged workers to dance on the grapes at a faster speed and provided the stompers with a musical focus to forget how tiring and difficult the job was. Biblical historian Arthur Klinck tells how they were allowed frequent breaks where they renewed their energy by drinking the wine of previous harvests and enjoying the fellowship of conversation, jokes and riddles. Compare this festive image with Isaiah's depiction of the isolated winepresser as an archetype of Christ's suffering, "I have trodden the winepress alone" (63:3). Jesus, abandoned by his three most trusted companions in the Garden of Gethsemane, also experienced oppressive suffering by himself.[7]

Of the Scripture's multiple wine-related images, some of the most telling are reserved to describe God's awful judgment, as found in Revelation 14:18-20:

> And another angel came out from the altar, the angel who has authority over the fire, and called with a loud voice to the one who had the sharp sickle, "Put in your sickle and gather the clusters from the vine of the earth for its grapes are ripe." So the angel swung his sickle across the earth and threw it into the great winepress of the wrath of God. And the winepress was trodden outside the city, and the blood flowed from the winepress, as high as a horse's bridle, for 1,600 stadia.

Contrast this with Isaiah 25, and God's universal summons to the banquet of salvation, "On this mountain the Lord of hosts will make for all peoples a feast of rich food, a feast of well-aged wine, of rich food full of marrow, of aged wine well refined" (v. 6).

And, of course, there is
Supper, that holy event of high
Church. There the essential n
and blood is hidden "in, with
feeble attempt to describe th
and wine, "Drink of it, all of y
of the covenant, which is po
the forgiveness of sins" (Matt
historian Paul Maier says, "V
inaugurated what became t
meal in history . . . ."[8] Upon
Jesus commits not to havin
until after his work here on
tell you I will not drink again
until that day when I drink
Father's kingdom" (Matthew
no respite, no pleasure until
finished. Christ's death and
that you and I, as forgiven ch
day share with him the frui
It is the promise to which we
until that day when God's pro
realized.

in order to determine if a wine is great. The first is the grape's distinct varietal character. MacNeil explains, "When a young wine that has been made from a single variety of grape presents its inherent grape aromas and flavors in a straightforward, clear and focused way, it is said to have varietal character."[9] My wife and I recently had that experience as we shared a 2009 Napa Valley Flying Horse Petit Verdot. Its distinct manure-like nose, which my wife discreetly described as "earthy," reminded us of a previous journey through the region of Bordeaux in the southwestern part of France. Its tart blueberry characteristics were unmistakable as well as pleasurable.

Wine connoisseurs (or should we say, wine snobs) speak a language that most of us can scarcely understand. For example, the varietal character of a good Chardonnay might be described as buttery, chewy, fruity, smoky, musty or full-bodied. A Meursault Chardonnay has a nutty flavor while a Chardonnay from Chablis might possess a hint of mineral. Some have compared the varietal character of Cabernet Sauvignon to dense blackberry, melted black licorice, cassis, coconut, chocolate, leather, crushed rock flavors, cinnamon, a cigar box, baking spice or a dash of espresso.

Such descriptors, as over-the-top as they may be, do serve a purpose; I find myself employing similar terms. For example, I have learned to shy away from Cabernets that have a fruity characteristic, favoring those with a more mineral, tobacco, smoky, and/or chocolate flair. However, on most days I adhere to the words of French vintner Michel Chapoutier, one of the world's most successful winemakers, who said: "If you think too much, you kill it."[10] This simple word of advice allows me to appreciate something about (nearly) every wine—a lesson I sometimes forget when interacting with my fellow human beings.

Every fan of the vine, like the wine they imbibe,

possesses his or her own style and flair. Descriptions often reflect one's personality. Journalist Auberon Waugh is unapologetic in his exhortation to avoid lukewarmness in one's descriptions, showing passion and creativity instead. In *Waugh on Wine*, he writes: "The [wine] writer should never like a wine, he should be in love with it; never find a wine disappointing but identify it as a mortal enemy, an attempt to poison him . . . . Bizarre and improbable side-tastes should be proclaimed: mushrooms, rotting woods, black treacle, burned pencils, condensed milk."[11]

Similarly, novelist and oenophile Jay McInerney affectionately describes a 1982 Haut-Brion as smelling "like a cigar box containing a Montecristo, a black truffle and a hot brick sitting on top of an old saddle. It's as earthy and complex as a Shakespearean sonnet."[12] That review immediately speaks to me, makes me yearn for just one sip at some point during my lifetime. Of course, not all identifiers have a pleasant connotation. Some disapprovingly have characterized a certain Cabernet as having the nose of a wet dog. Old running shoes is another descriptor a winemaker would prefer not to hear.

The question before us—staying with wine as a metaphor for faith and discipleship—is "What is our varietal character?" How might our spouse, child, co-worker or neighbor describe us using such terminology? Would our descriptors include a whiff of self-centeredness or the unpleasant aroma of a short temper? Or perhaps there is an overwhelming smell of material pursuit, while only a faint detection of concern for others.

There are aspects of all our lives which are, since we are sinners, in need of work. After prayerful discernment we are compelled to ask how we can maximize our personal "vintage." What actions might we incorporate in order to enhance our varietal character, to present ourselves to others for a more favorable review? Will our neighbors note the pleasing aroma of faith-in-action as we deliver dinner down the street to a family who recently suffered a loss? Does a co-worker notice anything different about our words or our behavior because we call ourselves Christian? Are we comfortable with our children imitating what we say and what we do? Will we be valued not for our successes and material possessions, but rather for having loving hands and a servant heart? The chances we have to help a stranger clean up after a natural disaster, to visit a friend in the hospital or to write a note of support to someone during a difficult time are just some of the daily opportunities we have to serve our neighbors.

An axiom of the wine trade is to "buy on the apple and sell on a cheese." The acid in the apple will reveal the flaws in a wine. Cheese, however, will complement the flavor of a wine; it provides a forgiving fatty layer between our taste buds and the apple's acidity, neutralizing the tannins with proteins.[13] This is what makes cheese the perfect accompaniment with wine, and why the smart host will serve it when entertaining with a less-than-perfect bottle. Likewise, the cheap party guest hopes there is cheese aplenty to cloak the first sip of the "gift" he proffers.

To draw yet another comparison (and to further stretch our metaphor), not even our best efforts can disguise the offensive nature of our sin to God. He is the most discriminating of hosts and demands nothing short of the finest vintage. Only the perfect offering of Christ's death and resurrection obliterates our offenses and meets God's requirements. This gift comes to us afresh in the wine and bread of the meal at worship. There our sins are forgiven, and from there we leave with our varietal character enriched. Out of humility and thankfulness we raise our glass up to the heavens in deep appreciation.

CHAPTER 5

Integration as a Strategy for Living

There is nothing better for them than to be joyful and to do good as long as they live; also that everyone should eat and drink and take pleasure in all his toil—this is God's gift to man.

Ecclesiastes 3:12-13

The second quality to consider when determining the greatness of a wine is integration. This is the result when a wine's various components—its acidity, tannin structure, alcohol content, fruitiness,

sweetness and/or dryness—are so impeccably interwoven that no one characteristic or component stands out. Integration denotes more than just balance; it also implies a healthy tension of opposites that "come together in harmonious fusion."[14]

Internationally known wine expert Hugh Johnson describes how wine needs to have balance, harmony and energy, "as though the wine were a living organism interacting with my tongue and palate."[15] Johnson draws a comparison to the world of music—how the various notes relate to each other to produce harmony or discord. What type of "volume" does the wine project, and what are the internal balances between volumes? He notes, "A brass chord may fill your ears, but a new phrase from the violin or a whisper from the woodwind will still catch your attention."[16] A Meursault white Burgundy comes to mind as a perfect example of such harmony.

To celebrate a Hong Kong publisher acquiring the rights to my most recent book, my wife and I shared a bottle of a 2008 Opus One that captured our imagination in this symphonic manner. A Robert Mondavi/Baron Philippe de Rothschild joint venture, this admittedly overpriced masterpiece uses a combination of Napa Valley Cabernet Franc, Cabernet Sauvignon, Merlot, Petit Verdot and Malbec grapes to produce a Bordeaux-Pauillac blend that lingered in our hearts, senses and imagination long after the bottle was emptied. The soothing combination was truly a gift for which we took time to pause, reflect and give thanks.

When drinking a fine wine, it is recommended that the glass be filled only halfway, leaving room to swirl the liquid and allow the oxygen thereby introduced to enhance the aroma and flavor, adding to the integration. There are times our lives, like an improperly poured glass of wine, lack integration and balance. The cumulative layering of managing deadlines and pressures at work, taxiing our children to after-school activities, answering one more email or caring for an elderly parent fills up our time, leaving no room for that which would enhance our lives. Like modern-day Marthas, we scurry from task to task, missing the "one good part" that brings harmony to our days.

In our striving to lead integrated lives we often need reminding that perfection will never exist this side of heaven. We lead both/and lives—broken and forgiven, selfish and generous, arrogant and humble. Having written a couple of books on this inherent tension in my Christian walk, and having been informed by family members and colleagues that I am a work in progress, I will refrain from giving a lecture. Suffice it to say, in my experience an integrated life is more of a blend than a balance. Blending occurs when we intuitively understand that all aspects of what I refer to as our vocation—our activities in family, professional, community and church spheres—are equally important. In our baptism we are recreated; that which had been out of balance is restored so that the spheres of our vocation interact and are mutually supported, rather than being used to compete and be in conflict. Integration also requires that we pay equal attention to both the doing and being aspects of our lives. It is as important to take time for spiritual renewal and personal revitalization as it is to reach out and serve others.

A life well lived is measured not by how much we do but by how well we do it. At every turn in our path are people to whom we can offer care in the name of Jesus. Integrated living is the natural by-product when we comprehend that we have been created to worship God and be of service to others. Only then will we experience—even in the midst of our hectic, stress-filled days—the peace that passes all understanding.

Proverbs 31 tells of a woman who successfully integrated the various aspects of her life. Authors Thomas Addington and Stephen Graves describe her as follows:

> This woman got high marks from the customers in all the key sectors of her life. In the family area . . . her husband had full confidence in her (v. 11) and her children called her blessed (v. 28). Her business associates recognized that she was a wise investor (vv. 16, 18), a conscientious employer (v. 15) and

a hard worker (v. 17). In her community, she was known for caring for the poor (v. 20), and she was praised at the city gate for her "works" (v. 31).[17]

Note especially verse 16: "She considers a field and buys it: From her profits she plants a vineyard." As much as I am in love with my wife, this may be the woman of my dreams. At a minimum, she serves as a role model for us all.

CHAPTER 6
Expressiveness

*What is the definition of a good wine? It should start
and end with a smile.*

William Sokolin

Wine is also judged by its expressiveness.
This is reflected by the definition and
clarity of its aromas and flavors. *The Wine
Bible* describes the distinction between a muddled
and diffuse wine versus one that has focus and clarity
as the difference between "an out-of-focus black-and-
white television without a cable hook-up compared to
the same image in high density color."[18] Famed wine
dealer Kermit Lynch adds that a good wine can express
itself aesthetically, spiritually, intellectually and

sensually. A good example is a New Zealand or French Sauvignon Blanc. Lynch, after tasting a series of French Sancerre Blancs, exclaimed, "Rather than leaving the impression that wine is simply another beverage,

they inspired the notion that wine can communicate something."[19]

It has been said that there are two types of wine drinkers: Old World and New World. If, for example, you prefer your wine to come from France, Germany, Italy or Spain, you are a fan of the Old World. Or are you a fan of California wines? Maybe your preference is wine from Australia, Missouri, Washington, Texas or even Chile? If so, then you are a fan of New World wines. My wife leans toward the New World and I somewhat to the Old. I love the clarity of an Old World wine's nose, of breathing in the aroma of its *terroir*—its location, place in history and mineral attributes. For just that brief period, I am transported to Bordeaux or the Piedmont region in Northern Italy. At such moments, the wine expresses itself as more than an average wine. My wife, on the other hand, enjoys the bold flavor of a Napa cult Cabernet, say a Hoopes or a Ghost Block. Both of us enjoy the grippy tannins of a good Argentinian Malbec or, when enduring the Texas heat, a French Rosé or an Italian Prosecco. Whether Old World or New World, we never fail to appreciate a wine that expresses its flavors and aromas distinctly and with clarity.

As a fine wine distinguishes itself from the not-so-fine bottles, we are called on to declare by our words and deeds that we are distinct among the crowd. Yet it is often difficult for us to express our faith with clarity. We develop surreptitious but effective methods by which we fit in with our colleagues for whom faith doesn't seem important. As a result, our words and actions become muddled, the expression of our faith lacks focus, and the beauty of Christ-in-us is veiled. Before we know it, we discover that we have allowed the distinctive nature of our Christian faith to become sullied; our lives no longer reflect the artisanal quality of our Creator or the clear call of our baptism. We quietly ask, "What happened?"

To be a Christian is to follow Christ, and that means being counter-cultural. Like the Good Samaritan in Jesus' parable, we must cross geographical, cultural and religious boundaries to help our hurting neighbor. Jesus reminds us in John 15:18-19 that we are not of the world, and that as Christians the world may indeed hate us. Similarly, the apostle Paul instructs, "Do not be conformed to this world, but be transformed by the renewal of your mind, that by testing you may discern what is the will of God, what is good and acceptable and perfect" (Romans 12:2).

It is through our baptism that we are transformed and are called to humility and service. We are driven to discomfort over the ways of the world that run counter to God's intentions. Dietrich Bonhoeffer reminds us that when we respond to God's call, we become divorced from our previous existence and create a new life for ourselves.[20] In this new existence we may never hear others describe us as rich, strong or sleek. Instead, our lives are marked by the fruit of the Spirit—love, joy, peace, patience, kindness, goodness, faithfulness, gentleness and self-control (Galatians 5:22-23).

CHAPTER 7
Complexity

I am the vessel. The draught is God's. And God is the thirsty one.

Dag Hammarskjöld

Another quality by which to judge a great wine is its complexity, a trait, according to *The Wine Bible*, that is not easy to describe, taste or hold on to. Like gravity, it is a force that compels you repeatedly to return for another taste, because with each sip you discover something new. *The Wine Bible* compares it to a movie that appears continually in your consciousness days after you have seen it.[21] I liken the trait of complexity to a great piece of art that stimulates numerous sensory perceptions. Wine

writer Jay McInerney describes it in a slightly different manner. He loves wines "that make me drool, that make me weak at the knees, that make the hair on the back of my arms stand at attention, that make me want to howl at the moon and kiss my girlfriend repeatedly."[22] A passionate description like this sets a high bar for any oenophile.

For me, complexity is all about a wine's finish. The longer its flavor and aroma linger, the better the wine. A well-aged Bordeaux or Napa Valley cult Cabernet come to mind. Or I think of the finish of a 2003 Dom Perignon I recently tasted and that still haunts. One connoisseur exclaimed after drinking a

Gamay wine from the Beaujolais region, "[Y]ou would need a *corniole* [gullet] as long as a swan's to make the pleasure last longer."[23] This review got my attention. It persuaded me to reassess my perception of the wine from this French region.

The wine of Communion, the very blood of Christ when taken and drunk in the company of believers, is still wine. And as an earthly substance, the taste of it remains when I leave the Table. The miracle embodied there is what makes me "weak at the knees" and wanting to shout with joy. It is ever a reminder of God's grace; it remains and will sustain me for the week ahead—for the rest of my life—until I share it with the whole communion of saints at the banquet feast in heaven.

Theologian William McElvaney captures that essence. When the Word has "become the cradle of our imagination, and the context of our illumination, and the content of our implementation, there is no telling what transformations God can bring about in individuals and society."[24] How might our lives change if we allowed God's Word to bring us to our knees? To make us howl at the moon? Like a fine wine that takes our senses to new heights, when we drink of the Scriptures, the Holy Spirit opens our eyes to the blessings and challenges of life and gives us power to transform our little corner of the world.

In a scene from the movie *Sideways*, Paul Giamatti, as Miles, a self-sabotaging oenophile, babbles on about the virtues of Pinot Noir with Virginia Madsen's character, Maya. It becomes apparent that his comments are an unconscious, thinly veiled reflection of himself in all his complexities which have yet to be discovered. There are times we have much in common with Miles. We let go—lose sight—of that which gives our life meaning and purpose, and which can be found only in God's Word. Then self-awareness evaporates. Only by looking at ourselves through the Scriptures can we know ourselves as we truly are—broken and forgiven people. As we grow and change, the Scriptures speak to us—work through us—in new ways. We become aware of our place in the world. Indeed, we are earthen vessels, as St. Paul says (2 Corinthians 4:7). Yet in our weakness the light of Christ shines through us. Like an artisan crafts a fine wine, the Holy Spirit continually shapes us, working through the fragile places in our lives to reflect the love of God to those around us.

While tasting a flight of French Brut champagnes recently, I was able to appreciate the aromatic, layered complexity of an orchard in late spring. It was gratifying to know that repeated exposure to and education about wine had begun to refine my palate (and much more work needs to be done). I like to think I have become more able to discern the complexities of God's Word through daily study—to appreciate the impact it has on my professional and family life, in both obvious and subtle ways. I experience the richness of meaning that comes with time spent in the Scripture as it soaks into my life, much as wine soaks into an oak barrel while being aged to perfection.

CHAPTER 8
Connectedness

But as for me and my household we will serve the Lord.

Joshua 24:15

Think of a Barolo from the Northern Italian region of Piedmont, with its striking aroma of tar and roses. Or the tart, acidic taste and perfume uniquely associated with a Riesling from the Mosel region of Germany. The name *Cote-Rotie* ("roasted slope") in the Northern Rhone region of France refers to an area of vineyards that receives long hours of sunlight which produce a wine that has a paradoxical bacon and floral smell and a savage peppery flavor.

Each of these examples speaks to the concept of connectedness, which *The Wine Bible* describes as the "bond between a wine and the plot of land it was born in,"[25] and is the final—and most elusive—quality for wine judging. A Riesling from Mosel is simply not the same as a Riesling from California.

Not every piece of land that is able to host a vineyard is also capable of giving a wine a recognizable and consistent character. Peter Sichel, the late vintner and wine merchant, described it this way: "The ultimate achievement in wine is to discover a *terroir* with a character potential." He goes on to say, "[I]f you are lucky enough to have a *terroir* that marks its wine with a memorable character, the last thing you should do is to adapt it to the market. You should educate the market to appreciate what it produces."[26]

Tradition can solidify the connectedness between a wine, a region and one's family. In certain regions of Spain, for example, *cava*—a Spanish version of champagne—is used ceremonially during the celebration of a baby's baptism. Guests raise a glass to toast the baby, whose pacifier is dipped in the bubbly. It has been said that other babies in attendance likewise partake, possibly as a strategy for keeping them quiet in church.[27]

Wine likely also played a role in the burgeoning relationship between Mary and Joseph. According to biblical historian Paul Maier, it would have been typical for Joseph's father, upon learning of Joseph's interest in marrying the village girl down the road, to visit Mary's parents to negotiate a covenant between the two families. Once the two fathers agreed to a marriage contract, Joseph and Mary would be brought together for a parental benediction, and the couple would sip from a common cup of wine. This formality resulted in a legal betrothal that was breakable only by divorce. So binding was this commitment—though not formally a marriage—unfaithfulness was considered to be adultery, and punishable by death.[28]

Reflecting on connectedness and tradition raises my appreciation for how the actions of my parents and ancestors have influenced my faith and life. It is daunting at times when my wife and I consider the responsibility we shoulder to bring up our daughter, Sydney, in the Word and in the world. I shudder to think of the possible ramifications on future generations should we fail in our intention to create a God-fearing, healthy marriage and family.

To place work over family or to become overly engaged in self-absorbed pursuits is to take the significance of family ties for granted. I have been humbled too often by that experience. Dietrich Bonhoeffer, writing from jail in 1943 on the occasion of a relative's wedding, reminds us of the beauty and import of God's gift of family:

> [Our home] is a kingdom of its own in the midst of the world, a haven of refuge amid the turmoil of our age, nay, more, a sanctuary. It is not founded on the shifting sands of private and public life, but has its peace in God. For it is God who gave it its special meaning and dignity, its nature and privilege, its destiny and worth.[29]

My wife and I celebrate the fellowship that has been created within and among the members of our family. That association of memory with meaning is not unlike the connectedness of an earthy Bordeaux with its geographical origin—the remarkable taste of the grapes and the aroma of that place remain in the wine. We savor family meals, multi-generational vacations, holiday celebrations, a shared faith and worship together. We know that these experiences are the ties that bind us to our Lord and will do so for generations to come as we follow his call to faithful and joyful living.

CHAPTER 9

What's in Your Wine Cellar?

This is the wine-cellar,
The place for the produce of the vine in it.
One is merry in it.
And the heart of him who goes forth from it rejoices.

Ancient Egyptian inscription
in a wine cellar at Esna[30]

Much to my chagrin, my wife and I don't have a wine cellar. We do have three climate-controlled wine refrigerators that hold approximately 140 bottles—more than enough for any normal couple (especially considering there

aren't many blizzards confining us to our Austin, Texas, abode). Because our preference continues to lean towards *vin rouge*, two refrigerators are devoted to reds and the other to whites. One "red" refrigerator houses our everyday drinking wines—Geyser Peak, McPherson, Rolling Meadows, Llano Estacado, as well as a variety of modest selections from Spain, Italy, Portugal, Argentina and Chile. The other "red" one holds our special and somewhat pricier vintages from South Africa, Spain, Washington, Oregon, California, Italy, Austria, Argentina and, of course, France, with a couple of port wines thrown in for good measure. Tempranillo, Cabernet, Pinot Noir, Sangiovese,

Malbec and Meritage blends are our grapes of choice. Current favorites include Chocolate Block from South Africa as well as a Steinbeck blend from Paso Robles. House sitters are well aware of which refrigerator is off limits. Our more savvy guests watch with anticipation the refrigerator we draw from when entertaining.

In the "white" refrigerator you will find a host of Proseccos and champagnes, along with some rosés (these aren't technically white, but appreciate the lower temperature). Mixed in are a few Old and New World Chardonnay and Sauvignon Blancs, as well as a couple of 1997 Rieslings from Mosel we are holding back for just the right occasion. The price range for our modest collection mostly spans from $12 to $60, with most bottles hovering at the lower end of the cost spectrum. Interspersed and well-hidden are several three-figure outliers—mostly gifts from very generous friends.

I share all this, not to brag about our private inventory, but as background for the question "What's in your cellar?" I am not referring to the one that houses your favorite beverage, but to something far more personal; it is the cellar that lies immediately beneath our public persona, where we hide our traits and weaknesses—some of which we aren't even aware.

To live out Christ's calling means in part to confront and acknowledge all of these. We like to appear to the world to be open, honest, fully functioning adults. The reality is there are nearly always certain thoughts and behaviors that remain subterranean.

Episcopal priest and author Morton Kelsey looks at the hidden stories behind the personas of three characters involved in the final days of Jesus. The Roman governor Pontius Pilate clearly didn't want to have to condemn Jesus to death by crucifixion. But he cared more about power and his comfortable station in life than he did about justice; he simply lacked the courage to do what was right. Another actor in the drama was Caiaphas, an admired and devout religious leader. Kelsey surmises that Caiaphas, although sincere in his intention, was too rigid in his understanding. He saw it as his duty to protect the people from this alleged troublemaker Jesus: "Far better for one person to die than for an entire nation to be destroyed," he reasoned (John 11:50). Finally, there was the nameless carpenter who built the cross, knowing how it would be used, but justifying his actions as those of a poor man merely trying to survive in a callous, brutal world.[31]

Which of these characters reminds us of

ourselves, who are unwilling to look in our own "cellars," the secret spaces in our lives? There, hidden next to the 1986 Lafitte Rothschild or the 2001 Dominus, are items of a much older vintage: greed that favors self-interest over the well-being of others, envy of another's talent that prevents us from appreciating our own gifts, an addiction that saps our energy for a higher purpose. Only when we allow light into the dark corners of our lives can we walk in the good works for which we were created (Ephesians 2:10).

I take comfort in knowing that heroes of the faith, too, have struggled with thoughts and behaviors that lurk beneath the surface of their lives. My personal hero is Dietrich Bonhoeffer, the German Lutheran pastor who gave up the security of living in the United States so that he could minister to the German people during the time of Hitler and who was ultimately killed in prison by the Nazis. In reading Bonhoeffer's *Letters and Papers from Prison*, it is evident that in some respects he was no different than you or me. He acknowledged having trouble writing unless he "smokes pretty hard."[32] He had bouts of insecurity, sickness and feelings of rejection. He became dejected and depressed, unable to be with family or participate in the rituals that family life entailed.

Yet even through Bonhoeffer's most intense periods of suffering and uncertainty he never compromised his pastoral responsibilities or lost sight of the beauty of God's creation, noting even the splendor of a bird singing in the prison courtyard. For him, the Christian faith can be lived out only in community. We experience God in our service to others, which flows from a baptism that is personal but never private. God does not watch over us from some distant heaven; he meets us in our daily lives—"in the middle of the village."[33] It is through personal suffering, and when we participate in the suffering of others, that we meet God. True faith, argues Bonhoeffer, must result in transformational consequences in the life of a believer; otherwise, it is what he would call "cheap grace." One cannot have faith without obedience or obedience without faith. Christianity, therefore, cannot be a lukewarm association that allows us to live as we choose. Rather, it demands uncompromising obedience, "a costly discipleship" in Bonhoeffer's language. Such a life is not a burden, but a path of joy, of mercy beyond measure.

Following Bonhoeffer's personal example of discipleship means detaching ourselves from the destructiveness of the world, feeding on God's Word and working to rid our lives of the vices that prevent us from following Christ. We cannot claim ignorance of those vices, for the Holy Spirit opens our eyes to see into the dark corners of our "cellars." We arise each day cleansed of our sin and empowered to respond to our baptismal call. It is an invitation, both terrifying and liberating, to live out our lives through prayer and service with honesty, humility and mercy.

CHAPTER 10
Terroir

To take wine into your mouth is to savor a droplet of the river of human history.

Clifton Fadiman

The French word *terroir* has no exact counterpart in English. It represents the totality of the location of a vineyard—its soil, elevation, slope, average high and low temperature, orientation to the sun, and frequency and amount of rain, wind and fog. To minimize the meaning of the word is to misunderstand its significance. In his observation about the Burgundy region of France, Hugh Johnson says *terroir* "explains the landscape, the culture, the economy, the social structure—even the folklore."[34]

This is but one example of the inadequacy of the English language to express the full significance of a word that other languages are able to convey. Earlier on, I commented on the term *vigneron*—the French word which, unlike the English "winemaker," captures the essence of the humble, close-to-the-earth role of a grape grower. The term reflects the idea that God and nature play a much more important role in the making of wine than we humans do. Similarly, the Spaniards use the verb *elaborer*, "to elaborate"—as opposed to the more pedestrian *fabricar*, "to produce" or "to manufacture"—to describe the winemaking process. From their perspective, *elaborer* is more exact in that it highlights the creativity and nurturing aspects of the wine process.[35]

Several years ago, my family and I had the privilege of traveling through the Burgundy region of France. We stopped in the historic villages of Pommard, Volnay, Meursault, Monthelie and Auxey-Durresses, among others, to sample their prized *vin rouge* and *vin blanc*. How good are the wines from Burgundy? Good enough to cause a serious diplomatic and religious incident in the 14th century, when the cardinals of the Catholic Church who were stationed in Avignon, France, refused to return to Rome because there were no Burgundy wines in Italy.[36]

At each of our stops we noted with fascination how the wines, made with the same grape in close proximity to each other and with virtually the same sun exposure, climate and time of harvest, could possess such a different taste and distinct character. A Pinot Noir from Volnay, for example, is lighter and more elegant than one from Pommard, which tends to be more powerful and tannic than its close neighbor. There is a slight variance in soil content and topography between the two geographies. But it is the creativity of the local *vigneron* that seems to account for the difference. Similarly, in the neighboring Loire

Valley, a Sancerre-based Sauvignon Blanc might come from limestone, flint or clay soil, each producing a remarkably different taste.

During our travels along the *vin route* of Burgundy, the conversation turned to the makeup of one's own *terroir*. Someone mentioned the Parable of the Sower:

> A sower went out to sow. And as he sowed, some seeds fell along the path, and the birds came and devoured them. Other seeds fell on rocky ground, where they did not have much soil, and immediately they sprang up, since they had no depth of soil, but when the sun rose they were scorched. And since they had no root, they withered away. Other seeds fell among thorns, and the thorns grew up and choked them. Other seeds fell on good soil and produced grain, some a hundredfold, some sixty, some thirty. He who has ears let him hear (Matthew 13:3-9).

There in Burgundy, I began to ponder the condition of my personal *terroir*. What soil am I planted in? My daily rituals of prayer and Bible study, the friends I keep, the person I marry, the habits I hide, the movies I watch and the profession I choose all are important aspects of the garden that is my life. But it is not my garden only that occupies my time. I must be aware of those around me, as all of us must. Are our children planted in the fertile soil of love and creativity? Are we sensitive to the plight of a friend or colleague whose *terroir* is showing signs of financial or emotional stress? These are legitimate questions that challenge and provoke.

An unfortunate trend in the wine industry is for a vintner to absolutely maximize each acre of the vineyard, to grow as many grapes as the land will allow. This is a by-product of the demand placed upon growers in a supermarket economy for low-cost wines. This currently is seen in places like the region of Coonawarra, Australia, where large conglomerates have swept in and replaced laborers with mechanical harvesters to produce "assembly wines." Australian vintner Brian Croser has this to say about the trend: "Of course a big leafy vine will give you lots of alcohol. Anyone can do that. But that is not why the names of French villages are world famous, and it is a total waste of a national asset like Coonawarra."[37]

Do we compromise our values by conforming to the demands of a market-minded society? Are we blending in with the world to the point of sacrificing the unique life to which God has called us? The prophet Jeremiah reminds us of the gracious nature of that call: "For I know the plans I have for you, declares the Lord, plans for welfare and not for evil, to give you a future and a hope" (Jeremiah 29:11). This future sets the stage for us as humble *vignerons* to use our gifts wisely.

Fortunately, there appears to be a nascent movement among some winemakers determined not to give up their souls in the process of tending their vineyards. For them it is more about their love for the work than just about producing a wine. One can almost taste and feel the humanity that goes into the making of their product.

We have a choice about how we live our lives. We can choose to "sell out" by making concessions that are not in keeping with our deepest values. Or, we can tend our vineyard faithfully, finding the sweet spot that combines personal integrity with the common good. This is where we discover our mission in the world. It is the path of faith that leads to a life of significance.

CHAPTER 11
The Grip of a Tannin

In wine, there's truth.

Pliny the Elder

To describe it in its simplest form, the tannin of a wine comes from the skins and seeds. Tannins contribute two properties to the character of a red wine—astringency and bitterness. Astringency refers to the dry, puckered feeling in your mouth after a sip of red wine. Hugh Johnson explains, "Tannins give wine texture, a 'grip' on the palate that can pinch like a shoe or scrape like sandpaper, but can also invigorate or caress, even invigorate *and* caress."[38]

This tannic characteristic can give the wine traction, a framework that allows the other flavors to express themselves. California Cabernet Sauvignons—Chalk Hill, Caymus and Pride, for example—come to mind as wines whose tannins are both noticeable and well-integrated.

To truly experience tannins in their purest form, you may want to try grappa. But be forewarned: it is an encounter you are not likely to forget. Grappa is popular throughout Italy, but especially in the north. This clear brandy is made from grape pomace (the pulpy mash of stems, seeds and skins leftover from winemaking) that has been re-fermented and

66

distilled. While some grappas are downright nasty (a gasoline quality comes to mind), others, such as the grappa di monovitigno, have a smooth, powerful taste that carries but a hint of the original grape's flavor. These expensive and hard-to-find grappas have created a feverish allegiance and cult-like worship among their followers. Enthusiasts are called *tifosi di grappa*, a phrase that signifies typhoid-like or feverish devotion.[39]

The "grippiness" of a tannin comes to mind when I consider how God binds himself to us in Holy Baptism. The sacrament transforms us essentially. It reveals to us a God worthy of highest commitment and praise. But there are times when our devotion might be described as timid at best. Would an observer characterize our walk of discipleship as a truly dedicated one? How obvious to others are the efforts of our Church to "Go therefore and make disciples of all nations . . . ." (Matthew 28:19). Where is the gusto with which we rally around our favorite sports team when it comes to serving those on the fringes of society? What is missing in our life that prevents us from living out a "feverish allegiance" to Christ?

In certain parts of Italy, the server will swirl a

small amount of wine in the glass, then discard the rinse before serving the patron. It is a baptism of sorts, preparing what might otherwise be a less-than-clean glass to receive the wine. I have taken up this custom at home (much to my wife's chagrin, given my propensity to spill). On one level, the practice recalls fond memories of our family's travels through Italy, as we wondered at the faith of the first martyrs in the Coliseum, explored the romantic vineyards of Tuscany or experienced grappa for the first time, surrounded by the majesty of the Italian lakes. On a more profound level, this simple rinsing ritual calls to mind my own baptism, and the knowledge that without it I would be ill-prepared for where life has led me. I humbly hold onto God's promise that he holds onto me, that I have been baptized for this moment, serving—at my better moments, with feverish intensity—those whom God has placed in my path.

CHAPTER 12
Wine and Family

*A man who could sit under the shade of his own
vine with his wife and his children about him and
the ripe clusters hanging within their reach in such a
climate as this and not feel the highest enjoyment is
incapable of happiness.*

James Busby

Novelist and oenophile Jim Harrison talks
about how difficult it is to make a truly
fine wine, given the innumerable variables
involved in the process. "The apprenticeship requires
the entire life," he observes. "You often have to wait
twenty years or more . . . to have any idea if art has
been 'committed.'"[40] When purchasing a vineyard, one

can't think of the product in terms of only a year or two, but must think in terms of generations. Typically, it will take 14 years from the time the first vine is planted until a vineyard makes a profit. That's if all goes well. Piero Antinori, whom some have referred to as the Robert Mondavi of Italy, once said about a piece of land he purchased, "This is a wonderful property; I think we will get our wines right in about four hundred years."[41]

The same concept holds true when it comes to creating and sustaining a family. This calling is a lifelong apprenticeship of service to the other. It entails a myriad of mundane acts of service to our spouse, children, parents, siblings, relatives—even our pets. It means washing clothes, shuttling children, caring for elderly parents, waiting up for teenagers to arrive home safely, wondering about financial security with an eye toward retirement, and coming together during times of crisis and celebration. Each of these is a lesson in setting aside our egos, learning from each other how to say "I am sorry" and forgiving graciously.

The path to "becoming family" is often a crooked one. Years, even decades, may pass before we can be sure that we have had a hand in creating something God-pleasing. And so we strive to lay the building blocks for a legacy that reflects our Christian faith, knowing that our decisions and acts of service today will impact future generations. Thus, our priorities change. We come to understand that relationships matter more than obtaining the latest toy and that money used for charitable causes makes a real difference in the world. We intuitively comprehend that spiritual formation is essential for our children to become caring and responsible adults, and we make decisions that reflect those values.

A consequence of living in a broken world is that family life is often messy and never easy. Likewise, even the most committed oenophiles will concede that creating wine isn't always the romantic undertaking as first envisioned. The nectar doesn't flow effortlessly from the vine to an elegant decanter, but is pumped unceremoniously through industrial-type hoses into barrels. As one laborer comments, "[It's] just like working in a refinery."[42]

We laborers in life's vineyard know that the work isn't always glamorous. There is pain, uncertainty and frustration along the way. We strive to establish some semblance of financial security in a changing economy that pressures us into a frenzied lifestyle. Work demands that we bring our job home—even on vacation sometimes—maintaining contact by cell phone and email. Such easy access to technology makes intimacy with family less compelling; we can "communicate" without ever having to lay eyes on the other person.

There is, of course, no turning back the clock on technological advancement—on the constant connectivity and the access to mountains of information it affords us. As CEO of an organization that operates numerous facilities that function around the clock, I am never completely off-duty. Balancing my commitment to work and my call to family is an ever-moving target that requires careful gauging. As part of my ongoing discernment process, I must frequently ask, "Where is the level at which my commitments at work exceed my responsibility to my family? At what point do I begin compromising long-term outcomes at home?" When I no longer like the answer (which is more often than I care to admit), I must make a conscious choice to "repack" my work-related bag in order to make more room for those I love.

I have learned that to be human is to be familial. Family provides us with our true identity, and the rituals we create reinforce that identity for our children. They grow up learning how their families celebrate the holidays, for example. The patterns we establish transcend the moment and reinforce what is truly important.

Traditions are often culturally conditioned. In Spain, for example, it is common for families to allow their young children to have a small glass of wine with dinner. Making it an incidental act in this way folds it naturally into the "main event," which is the coming together of family around the table. In other words, it's not about drinking alcohol, but about the perpetuating of a ritual that has helped shape their identity. It's hard to argue with this custom. Numerous

studies show that the more often a family eats together, the less likely their children are "to smoke, drink, do drugs, get depressed, develop eating disorders and consider suicide, and the more likely they are to do well in school, delay having sex, eat their vegetables, learn big words and know which fork to use."[43]

Anthropologist Robin Fox states succinctly how having our meals together as a family deeply affects our souls: "A meal is about civilizing children. It's about teaching them to be a member of their culture."[44]

Some families, including ours, incorporate wine as a thread in the fabric of their makeup. My daughter often engages in conversation with my wife and me as we enjoy a glass in the interlude between the day's busy-ness and the sharing of our meal. She has learned that the quality of family is determined more by the character of our relationships than by the number of activities we engage in. And she knows that faith has been our unfailing compass. My daughter jokes that many of our family vacations end by visiting a winery or two. But beneath the joking, she has seen that alcohol can be consumed intelligently and in moderation—that it is not a mystery, but one of God's gifts that enriches our life together. We continue to enjoy pictures of my daughter at a young age, sitting in a chair in the corner of a tasting room, patiently reading a book, as she waits for her slightly crazed parents to find the perfect wine for the evening meal.

As we watch our daughter mature as a young adult, sharing a bottle of wine has become our "prescription of choice" to help create a rare quiet evening at home—a place of refuge away from a day of frenzy. It allows us space to slow down, take a breath, settle in and just be with each other.

CHAPTER 13

Wine and Children

There is truth in wine and children.

Plato

Wine often goes through what is called a "dumb phase," a period where its taste has very little depth or charm. In Bordeaux, this is referred to as its *age ingrat*, or difficult age. It is a phenomenon every parent can relate to. Fortunately, it's not a permanent condition. Every wine—and, we pray, every child—at different points in time turns the corner and heads toward maturity.[45]

Making wine, like rearing children, is a blend of art, faith and science. You have to know each vine intimately, when to baby it and when to withhold water to provide the stress necessary to produce abundant flavor. Sometimes hardcore science is involved—decisions about fermentation, for example. Other times, you simply have to go with your gut instinct, choosing just the right time to harvest the grape, or in the case of children, when to give them their freedom, even if you aren't quite ready.

Among the qualities integral to raising a well-adjusted child is hard work, which includes stress, when introduced in appropriate and measured forms. Curiously, most of the world's great vineyards are in locations that are less than ideal for this purpose. A certain degree of adversity, due to climate, topology or any number of other factors, causes the grapevine to struggle and adapt. A Syrah, for example, appears to benefit from wide temperature swings that stress the vine. Too much stress can wither and kill the vine. An appropriate amount, however, forces plants to "concentrate their sugars in a limited number of grape clusters," which ultimately provides us with "wine of greater character and concentration."[46]

More important than the toys and other distractions we provide our children is the kind of environment we create for them. A son learns by watching how his father treats his mother. A daughter sees that breadwinning and homemaking can be the proper functions of both mother and father. Here again, winemaking offers a metaphor. The cellar in which a wine ages has an obvious impact on the end product. Compare, for example, the difference between the finish and complexity of a wine stored in a cavernous cellar versus that of a wine kept in a stainless-steel tank that sits outside many of today's vineyards. Kermit Lynch explains the difference: "Underground there is a confluence of factors beneficial to a healthy evolution: the cold temperature, the humidity, the mineral walls . . . . [T]here you have the constituents of a good cellar: low temperature, humidity, earth and wood smells." He goes on: "As in rearing a child, the details of a home environment form a wine's character."[47]

Mother Teresa once observed about the United States, "In your country you have an even bigger problem [than hunger]. So many of your children are starved for love and affection."[48] For a time, our daughter babysat for a very wealthy family. Their children seemed to have everything. They lived in a castle-like mansion, complete with its own elevator. They had a full-time nanny, a cook and even a live-in personal trainer. Dad traveled globally as a Fortune 500 executive, while much of Mom's time was eaten up by various pursuits. My daughter was paid to care for the three children when the nanny wasn't present. Coming home from her job one evening, she commented, "Dad, these kids have everything, but they aren't happy. All they want is for their parents to pay attention to them." She added, with a smile, "Our home sure is small compared to theirs, but I think I would rather live here."

The French word *elevage* has no direct English equivalent. In its literal sense, *elevage* means "rearing" or "raising." When someone says that a child is *bien eleve*, it means he or she is "well brought up." When used to describe the production of wine, the word refers to the series of decisions and cellar operations that occur between the stages of fermentation and bottling—the time after the grape's harvest, which includes the aging of the wine in oak barrels. It suggests that a winemaker's role is much like that of a parent who instructs, guides and civilizes the young wine that emerges from the fermentation vessel. Typically, *elevage* is used only when referring to a quality wine, as the word implies that the effort is worth the time and expenditure. As Hugh Johnson notes, the French lovingly speak of their wine as we in the English-speaking world refer to our children.[49] The *vigneron* knows each barrel of wine in his cellar as if it were his own child, memorizes the age, perceives the potential, notices every change of smell or appearance—and provides the conditions necessary for the grapes under his care to flourish.

It is helpful for me to think of my role as a father as that of a *vigneron*, just as God is my Father and *Vigneron*. God's love knows no bounds. He has given us fruitful *terroir*, a landscape that has been shaped by a history of sins forgiven and promises fulfilled. We blossom, not as under the hand of an inattentive vine-dresser, but under the caress of One who knows us intimately. The family in which God has placed us is made up of a variety of relationships and to follow this vocational call according to his plan is an invitation we are free to accept or refuse. We strive to raise our child, foster child or grandchild as *bien eleve*—well brought up. That involves effort and intention on our part. No doubt we will make missteps and mistakes along the way. But we are comforted and strengthened by God, as *Vigneron*, who will not leave us to wander too far or to wither.

CHAPTER 14

Generosity of Spirit

Wine to me is passion. It's family and friends. It's warmth of heart and generosity of spirit. Wine is art. It's culture. It's the essence of civilization and the art of living.

Robert Mondavi

The production of wine is a microcosm of all that is good and bad in our global economy. During harvest in Napa and Sonoma, thousands of Mexican workers are camped everywhere, out of tourists' sight. The plight of the day laborer is striking in contrast to the chateaus that

dot the countryside and the limousines that cruise Highway 29, transporting guests to the next tasting stop. This person might work ten hours to earn what a white-collar professional spends for one designer-label bottle of wine. Some vineyard owners now offer wine camps, where one pays upwards of $1,000 to have the experience of picking grapes shoulder-to-shoulder with laborers who have been stooping since long before daybreak to earn $2 for each bucket they fill. When asked what the migrant workers think of this phenomenon, one camp counselor said, "They think gringos loco."[50] This, sadly, is the picture of the wine industry in America.

The wine industry in times past has proven to be more than merely a vendor of product. Fifteenth-century Burgundy, home to rolling expanses of vineyards and castles, was an epicenter of wealth and culture. Erasmus of Rotterdam once noted enthusiastically, "Oh happy Burgundy, worthy of being called mother of humanity, since from its breast gushes forth such exquisite milk."[51] Its citizens also took their commitment to serve the least of these seriously. It was in Beaune, the region's wine-producing center, where in 1443, Nicolas Rolin, chancellor to the Duke of Burgundy, and his wife, Guigone de Salins, founded the Hotel-Dieu Hospital for the sick and indigent.[52]

The monasteries in Europe have long been known for their fine wine. Over the centuries, monks honed the art of winemaking to maintain a steady supply for use in the Mass. In 1510, a Benedictine monk named Dom Bernando Vincelli first distilled wine at the monastery in Fecamp on the Normandy Coast. On each bottle he placed the letters D.O.M.— *Deo Optimo Maximo*: To God, the Best, the Greatest. Monks often used the money raised from the sale of the surplus wine after Mass to provide for the sick and the destitute.

But not even monks are perfect. It was in the 10th century that two monastic orders, the Abbey of Cluny and, later, the Abby of Citeaux, formed in the Burgundy region. Monks cleared the ground and replanted the vine-stock, laying the groundwork for the product Burgundy is most known for today. By the 14th century, the monks there had come to enjoy the results of their labor a little too much, leading the townspeople to create a stinging jingle:

> To drink like a Templar [a knight of a military religious order] is to drink heartily,
> To drink like a Franciscan is to empty the cellar.[53]

The account serves as a warning that even those who spend their days in service to others can overindulge and abuse God's gift.

Today communities like Napa, Sonoma and a host of others continue the tradition of giving back. Auction Napa Valley, the annual fundraiser sponsored by the Napa Valley Vintners, has raised more than $100 million to help provide health care, youth services and affordable housing in the community. You and I may not have the deep pockets to bid thousands of dollars on a case of the valley's highly sought-after cult wine, Screaming Eagle. But each of us does have the resources—if not financial, perhaps in sweat equity or by a caring presence—to volunteer at the local thrift shop or to help build a well for water in Ethiopia. In whatever setting we find ourselves, to whatever professional or volunteer arenas our passion leads, we can strive to make the quality of our work deserving of the stamp D.O.M. We offer to God the best and the greatest, in our being and in our doing—a return on the investment of grace he has made in us.

CHAPTER 15
Wine and Money

Honor the Lord with your wealth and with the first fruits of all of your produce; then your barns will be filled with plenty and your vats will be bursting with wine.

Proverbs 3:9-10

Outrageous stories abound about the purchase, storing and drinking of wine as a status symbol. Business executives compete to build the largest cellars. Chinese tycoons adapt easily to the excesses of capitalism, purchasing expensive French wines like they might Swiss watches or luxury cars. Exorbitantly priced champagne is pushed in domestic and foreign markets, creating a ready field

on which the wealthy find new ways to one-up their peers. Wineries have long understood that consumers often make purchases based not on taste so much as bragging rights. In a recent study, subjects were asked to rate two wines, each priced differently. They weren't told that the samples were the same wine. The tasters overwhelmingly chose the more "expensive" wine.[54]

Financial and ethical considerations about the cost of wine confound those concerned about equitable use of our resources. I struggle (more often than I care to admit) to justify my passion for wine when there are so many suffering people in the world. From the work I do, I am well aware that the cost of a single bottle would buy food for a child in a developing country for a week or even a month. My wife and I recently shared a $36 bottle of a fine Cabernet with our pastor and friend, Pete, on a beautiful spring Texas evening. It was a perfect accompaniment to our mutual sharing of the struggles and successes of the week. Yet my conscience still bothers me, wondering if the evening wouldn't have been just as enjoyable over a less expensive wine.

Discussion about the use of personal resources in the context of discipleship can make us uneasy. I turn to the Bible for guidance, and there I am faced with Jesus' disturbing pronouncement to the lawyer that he is to sell everything, give the money to the poor and follow him (Mark 10:17-22). I am further troubled by his alarming statement that it is easier for a camel to go through the eye of a needle than it is for a rich person to get into heaven (Matthew 19:24). And in the Parable of the Last Judgment in Matthew's Gospel, I shrink from reading that the sheep and the goats are separated based on how they treated the hungry, the sick and those in prison. As I noted in a previous book, *The Calling: Live a Life of Significance*, living in this society only intensifies our struggle. We are surrounded by messages that tell us we "own" our wealth, and that it is only out of the goodness of our hearts that we "generously" share any tidbits from our bounty with those less fortunate.

The Scriptures teach throughout that we are to use our material blessings for the good of the community, particularly those less fortunate than we are. God, through his prophet Moses, tells the people of Israel:

> When you reap the harvest . . . [d]o not go over your vineyard a second time to pick up the grapes that have fallen. Leave them for the poor and the alien. I am the Lord your God (Leviticus 19:9-10).

We are not, by our stewardship, gaining favor with God or earning our way to heaven. Our generosity finds its source in God's generosity to us. To quote Goethe's *Faust*, "What you have received as gift, you must take as task."[55]

By biblical standards, probably everyone who reads this book is rich. We have a roof over our heads, a private mode of transportation, the means to travel, a retirement plan and some form of health care. Richard Hays, author and New Testament professor at Duke University, urges us to think about our resources in the framework of community, cross and new creation. We are to act in community—to live together as followers of Christ that we may be seen as a city on a hill. From there, our good works shine both as a sign of God's glory and as a demonstration to the world of our faith. Hays points next to the notion that we are to carry the cross. Christ's ultimate surrender demands of us—makes it possible for us— to participate in self-sacrificial love toward others. Finally, life in Christ means using our resources as evidence that we live in a new creation where economic concerns and insecurities are secondary to seeking God's kingdom.[56] Hays says, "We are freed to act with a generosity that figures forth God's good future" and a "sharing that prefigures the joy and justice of the world to come."[57]

Only in God does life have meaning and pleasure, and the appropriate response to this gift of life is generosity. Mary, sister of Martha, is a role model for us all. During a visit from Jesus to her home, Mary anoints his feet with expensive perfume and wipes them with her hair. Judas took offense at what he perceived as an unjustified waste of resources that could have been given to the poor (a thin disguise, as it turns out, for his selfish motives). Jesus commends Mary's gesture as a sign that she had her priorities straight; it was a display not of carelessness, but of genuine worship. The story challenges us to rethink the criteria that order our priorities.

Mary could hardly afford this exorbitant display of faith. But there are biblical characters who could and did use their assets in service to God. Joseph, a rich man of Arimathea, placed Jesus' body in his own tomb (Matthew 27:57-61); Zacchaeus, a wealthy tax collector, gave half of his possessions to the poor and returned to those he had defrauded four times the amount of his larceny (Luke 19:1-10); Lydia, a businesswoman whose heart was opened to hearing God's Word, provided hospitality to Paul and his partners in ministry (Acts 16:13-15).

Daily we encounter opportunities to use our resources for the good of others and to the glory of God. I reflected on this recently upon returning from my church body's triennial convention. Much good was accomplished there as faithful men and women gathered, discussed and voted on a number of issues to benefit the Church. I also mused that there may be more than a little truth to this Italian proverb: "One barrel of wine can work more miracles than a church full of saints." In the work I do, wine has played a minor role in bringing donors together to support the important ministries of Lutheran Social Services. I recall a late evening in Geneva, Switzerland, when my friend John Nunes and I—a bottle of wine spurring the imagination—developed a strategy and sealed the deal on how to mobilize the faith community to help eradicate malaria. Wine was also occasionally on hand in the process of forging a partnership with Brad Hewitt, CEO of Thrivent Financial. The result of these collaborative efforts among Brad, myself and a number of others was a solid plan to strengthen and expand the mission of the organization.

Let our vision for using our resources in God's service embrace the community in all its shapes and sizes. Let us become rich in good works, for the fruit that we bear is evidence that, as vines to the branch, so are we connected to Christ, the source of life.

CHAPTER 16

Stepping Off Life's Treadmill

Wine makes daily living easier, less hurried, with fewer tensions and more tolerance.

Benjamin Franklin

Old World or New, it is becoming harder to find vineyards that focus exclusively on creating a truly complex, expressive wine. Increasingly, decisions are based on what is efficient, popular and profitable. Even in the Loire Valley and in much of the Bordeaux region, there has been a shift away from the fermenting of wine in wood barrels to stainless-steel containers. Sometimes vineyard owners are seduced

by their own success. A bottle rated at 90-plus by *Wine Spectator* emboldens a winery to overproduce. In order to meet its growing demands, owners may plant on less desirable sites or, following a secret purchase from a neighboring vintner, blend in grapes of a lower quality. The cycle is one of irony: the recognition of a quality product leads ultimately to the cheapening of it.

A similar dynamic is at work in the choices we make as human beings. At stake, however, is something far more valuable than a good bottle of wine. In a culture of consumerism, we are constantly driven

CHAPTER 17

To Our Health!

No longer drink only water, but use a little wine for the sake of your stomach and your frequent ailments.

1 Timothy 5:23

E ven the etymology of the word denotes the health properties of wine: *vitis* (the vine) and *vita* (life)—wine is life. The biblical reference above shows Paul's concern for his friend and colleague, Timothy. It was thought at the time that wine could prevent illness brought on by parasites or bacteria. Likewise, it was by "pouring on oil and wine" that the Good Samaritan provided roadside assistance to the wounded man (Luke 10:34). Presumably, oil was used to soothe and wine served as an antiseptic. While it disease among the French, who regularly consumed red wine.[65]

Today medical research indicates that a glass or two of wine per day can improve one's overall health. Various studies have demonstrated that red wine in particular, beyond its healthful benefits related to cardiovascular disease, can help reduce the risk of prostate cancer and kidney dysfunction. It can also contribute to relieving arthritis pain, staving off the flu and may even play a part in preventing hearing loss.[66] Researchers identified antioxidants—molecules beneficial to our health—in the seeds and skins of the grape. Because red wines have more contact with the skins and seeds during the winemaking process than white wines do, they are richer in antioxidants. A simple rule of thumb is, the darker the color of the wine, the more antioxidants it has.[67] It also appears that younger wines contain higher levels of antioxidants than older. If health is our focus, it stands to reason that we should focus our wine selection on Cabernets, Barolos and perhaps Bordeauxs, with a vintage of no more than five years. This is a medical prescription I can live with.

History, of course, also reveals the detrimental effects of wine caused by its abuse. Winston

Churchill, who was known to enjoy a drink (or four), in characteristic incisiveness notes, "A single glass of champagne imparts a feeling of exhilaration. The nerves are braced; the imagination is stirred, the wits become more nimble. A bottle produces the contrary effect. Excess causes a comatose insensibility."[68] We are all familiar with the adverse consequences of drinking too much alcohol, from a morning-after headache or the memory of a regretful comment, to the destructive repercussions of a drunk-driving charge, a broken marriage or the loss of a job. The law dictates how much alcohol is too much when in public or behind the wheel of a car. The responsibility for setting personal limits on our drinking lies with each of us, and should take into account such factors as age, health, genetic disposition to alcoholism and tolerance level. I subscribe to the philosophy of Dr. Murray Susser of the Longevity Center in Los Angeles: a couple of glasses of wine several days a week is of less consequence to the body than the benefits it provides the soul.[69]

Longevity of life is not our ultimate goal as Christians. The length of our days is a blessing from God, and our days are to be measured by the breadth and depth of our actions. There is a paradoxical element to the life of faith. We are to take care of our bodies, for they are temples of the Holy Spirit. At the same time, we are called to sacrifice ourselves on behalf of the hungry, hurting and infirm. To paraphrase theology professor Abigail Rian Evans, we have the privilege to become broken so that others may become whole. There is risk involved in this kind of living; it depletes our physical, emotional and spiritual energy. The older we get, the more tired we become. For French actress Brigette Bardot, the antidote was champagne. On approaching the age of 50, she said it is "the one thing that gives me zest when I feel tired."[70] We, too, might enjoy a sip of champagne—or whatever drink calls to us—as an occasional pick-me-up. But this is a passing pleasure. What remains is the nectar of God's Word—that which we read, we hear and we ingest at the Table of our Lord. There he reveals himself to us as "living water," the giver of abundant life that has no end. And from there we depart, our sins forgiven and our flagging spirits renewed.

CHAPTER 18

Suffering and the Vine

I am the vine, you are the branches. Whoever abides in me and I in him, he it is that bears much fruit, for apart from me you can do nothing. If anyone does not abide in me he is thrown away like a branch and withers; and the branches are gathered, thrown into the fire and burned. If you abide in me, and my words abide in you, ask whatever you wish, and it will be done for you.

John 15:5-7

To paraphrase a friend, "A branch doesn't have to work very hard to grow grapes, but it does have to stay connected to the vine." We get our succor from God. I take to heart the exhortation in Psalm 34, verse 8: "Oh, taste and see that the Lord is good!" Consider for a moment how one experiences a glass of good wine—noticing the richness of color, reading the label, smelling the cork, carefully pouring and swirling it in the glass, taking a deep whiff to experience its "nose," tasting it on the tongue and allowing it to linger in the mouth before swallowing. Reading the Bible is like drinking deeply of an exquisite wine. We exclaim with the composer of Psalm 42 that our soul "thirsts for God" (v. 2), and rediscover with each sip that his Word satisfies our deepest need.

When nourished by its source, an offshoot blossoms; its fruit is the natural result of its relationship to the vine. Just so, our words and actions reflect the nature of our relationship with God, evidence that we are connected to the source. "For we are his workmanship," the apostle Paul writes, "created in Christ Jesus for good works, which God prepared beforehand, that we should walk in them" (Ephesians 2:10). Christ works through us by asking us to serve as his hands and feet on earth—to be productive in our daily lives.

There are times, however, when we are not so bountiful, when we wither and are in danger of becoming detached from the source of life. Then we are dead wood, good only for kindling. Responsible owners must prune, chop, tear and pinch, not only to avoid that fate, but to demonstrate the hope they have that the vine will flourish once again. That process isn't always pleasant.

The life of discipleship necessarily entails suffering, the purpose of which is rarely understood and hardly ever appreciated. As Christians, we are called to embrace our suffering. This doesn't mean we are to have a martyr complex. Rather, it reveals our commitment to the One who suffered for us. Jesus' life, death and resurrection turn the conventional understanding of life's travails upside down. Hardships, failures and losses, rather than being seen as punishment, can be opportunities for the growth of our spirit. Martin Luther reminds us that there are two times in our life when we come closest to knowing God: when we suffer personally and when we focus on the suffering of Jesus. By becoming one of us in the person of Jesus, God chose to participate in our suffering. To paraphrase Luther, suffering is nothing less than our living God working out his salvation in our lives.[72]

Tribulation drives us to the cross and to the empty tomb, where our faith was born and from where we get our strength to persist. There we see evidence of Christ as the Suffering Servant. We are given grace to resist temptation and the strength to see it through. Adversity, when experienced in the context of our faith, reminds us that we servants are not greater than the Master. Out of crisis comes a re-ordering of priorities and fresh opportunities for service. There is a sense in which the Christian can think of suffering as one of God's alien "gifts," for it reminds us that, as

St. Paul says, God's strength is made perfect in our weakness (2 Corinthians 12:9). Strange as it sounds, our spiritual life is rooted in defeat—not as an end in itself, but as the path that leads to ultimate victory.

The Gospel of Christ animates us for holy living. By it, we come to know the peace that passes all understanding and are given the grace to be content in any circumstance. When we remain in Christ, every encounter with another person becomes a lesson in the practice of love.

CHAPTER 19

The Lord's Supper

And likewise the cup after they had eaten, saying, "This cup that is poured out for you is the new covenant in my blood."

Luke 22:20

Wine has always played an important role in the history of humankind in religious ritual, joyful celebration—even raucous debauchery. Bacchus (also known as Dionysus), the god of wine and mad religious ecstasy in early Greek and Roman society, was considered to be a "liberator." Those who participated in the wine drinking and

frenzied dancing of the Bacchanal feasts were considered to be possessed and empowered by the god himself and freed of their fears and cares. The intoxicating properties of wine allowed its followers to shed all inhibition and become one with the divine—a ritual that is played out in Mardi Gras festivities today.[73] It is conjectured by one school of thought that the miracle of Jesus turning water into wine at the wedding of Cana was to signify that "a greater god of wine had arrived than either Dionysus or Bacchus."[74]

Wine has often been paired in literature with some form of bread. The first such reference in the Bible occurs in Genesis, when King Melchizedek offers bread and wine to Abraham upon his return from victory in battle. It was a seal of friendship and blessing. One can trace similar traditions in different cultural expression down through the centuries until today. A snack consisting of bread dipped in wine is a favorite among children in Spain. In Italy, the mixture of wine (sprinkled with sugar), bread and olive oil make up the *Santa Trinita Meditarranea*, or Mediterranean Holy Trinity.[75] Wine author Gerald Asher notes, "[T]he longstanding affinity between bread and wine needs no emphasis . . . . The gesture of offering bread and wine is an ancient and hallowed prelude to hospitality, one we've transmuted into a glass of champagne and a canapé."[76]

For Christians, the association of bread with wine claims highest place and deepest meaning in the Lord's Supper. According to the Gospel account, Jesus, on the way to his triumphant entry into Jerusalem, sent Peter and John ahead to make arrangements for the Passover meal—the last he would share with the disciples before his crucifixion. The meal probably consisted of unleavened bread, bitter herbs and roast lamb.[77] Toward the end of the meal, Jesus instituted the singular event that forever identifies his Church on earth. He took the remaining bread "and after blessing it broke it and gave it to them, and said, 'Take, this is my body.' And he took a cup, and when he had given thanks he gave it to them, and they drank of it. And he said to them, 'This is my blood of the covenant, which is poured out for many'" (Mark 14:22-24). Biblical historian Paul Maier writes:

> With these words, Jesus inaugurated what became the longest continuous meal in history, for soon his followers would start celebrating what they later called The Lord's Supper or Holy Communion, in which someone, somewhere in the world, has been offering up bread and wine in a similar manner nearly every moment since.[78]

In the miracle of the meal instituted on the Thursday night of Passion Week, we receive—along with the bread and wine—the very body and blood of Christ that he would shed the next day as the sacrificial Lamb of God foretold by the prophets. This Gift of love for the world makes life with God—once lost because of sin—possible again. We leave our sins and grief at the altar of his Table, and come away having been forgiven and healed. The kind of wine a church uses for Communion is beside the point; red or white, sweet or dry, its taste will fade over time. What remains is the gift of Christ's love, which in the meal sustains us until we share it with him at the marriage feast in heaven.

Sixteenth-century French humorist and writer Rabelais wrote that wine is the symbol of life and hidden truth: *in vino veritas*. As we ponder the miracle of the Lord's Supper, and the ultimate sacrifice of our Lord it reveals, we are humbled at the knowledge that in this simple meal is hidden eternal life and ultimate truth. It is beyond our grasp why God would choose the simple earthly elements of bread and wine to convey the riches of his grace. In doing so, however, he has surely elevated the fruit of the vine as unique among all human libations.

CHAPTER 20

Christ's Death and Resurrection

*And when they came to a place called Golgotha,
they offered him wine to drink, mixed with gall, but
when he tasted it, he would not drink it.*

Matthew 27:33-34

When Jesus had completed the long, torturous walk to Golgotha, but before being nailed to the cross, he was offered wine mixed with gall. Tradition has it that the women of Jerusalem offered the numbing concoction as a humane effort to dull the pain that awaited prisoners about to be crucified. After Jesus tasted it, he refused to

drink it so that he could remain fully conscious until his death.[79] A while later, before taking his last breaths from the cross, he cried, "I am thirsty" (John 19:28). A jar of wine vinegar was available, so they soaked a sponge in it, placed it on a stalk of a hyssop plant, and lifted it to Jesus' lips (v. 29). This wine vinegar was the drink of ordinary people, equivalent to today's cheapest wine. The Gospel account continues: "When he received the drink, Jesus said, 'It is finished.' With that, he bowed his head and gave up his spirit" (v. 30).

There is, of course, no analogy in the wine world that can do justice to the holy suffering of Christ or capture the depth of our sin that was the cause of this atrocity. Reflecting on the drama of this scene, I return in my mind's eye to an area just south of Bordeaux, and there find a sparse analogy. This region is home to the famed—if overpriced—Margauxs, Lafite-Rothschilds and Latours. Some excellent sweet wines, such as Sauternes and Barsacs, are also born here, just south of Bordeaux, along the Garonne River. To produce this sweet wine the *vigneron* leaves Semillon and sometimes Sauvignon Blanc grapes on the vine well into the fall. The intent is that the grapes become infected with *pourriture noble*, or noble rot. These decaying grapes turn into furry, moldy raisins that ultimately become a magnificent wine that tastes like liquefied honey.[80] On the rare occasion when I partake of a glass of Sauternes, I am reminded of the miracle that God has transformed me from shriveled sinner to blossoming saint.

God reveals himself to us most clearly in the death and resurrection of Christ. The void our sin creates, separating us from God, is only filled by the divine grace that flows to us through the cross and the empty tomb of Jesus. His willingness to suffer on our behalf is the ultimate sacrifice and is the perfect demonstration of what it means to be truly obedient unto death. We are beneficiaries of this gift by faith—never by our good deeds. In the sixth chapter of Romans, Paul says that in baptism we are buried with Christ in death in order that we might be raised, like him, to newness of life (v. 4). Martin Luther makes much of this remaking of our nature, calling us "little Christs"—new creations enabled and ennobled by the Holy Spirit to do God's work of serving a hurting world.

CHAPTER 21
Savor and Serve

Wine is as old as the thirst of [humanity], not the physical thirst . . . but the heaven-sent thirst for what will stir our fear–that our mind will be at peace; and stir our sense and sensibility–that we shall not ignore or abuse God's good gifts–wine not the least of them.

Andre L. Simon

There is an old German saying: "Drink wine and you will sleep well. Sleep and you will not sin. Avoid sin, and you will be saved. Ergo, drink wine and be saved."[81] No doubt, the theology here is suspect. Still, I find there is something uniquely comforting and symbolic, spiritually, about the role wine plays in my life here on earth. Increasingly, the

journey is marked by an appreciation for a gracious God to worship and serve, family and friends to love, old prophets to learn from and new people to care for.

For me, my "dance" with the gift of wine has become an elegant window on my soul. It is an earthly touchstone that has enriched my gratitude for all of life, and—if I may use an admittedly unrefined concept here—lubricates my faith, marriage, family life, friendships and work. After spending eight, ten or even more hours in the day's pressure-cooker, a glass of wine can be therapeutic, even renewing, as we experience these finest qualities the Bible ascribes to it. On a more personal level, it lets this city dweller reconnect with the stuff of creation and recall the wonders of the God behind it all.

Bonds are forged, fellowships are renewed and plans are laid when people gather around a meal and a bottle of wine. This oldest and simplest form of fellowship relaxes, inspires and makes possible the elusive escape from trials and tribulations—if only for an evening. We create, we heal, we celebrate, we rest and, come morning, we rise—as if from the waters of our baptism—refreshed to meet the new day. Living the Christ-filled life is to be intoxicated with the Gospel. We learn anew that life without God leaves us with a yearning emptiness that the finest bottle from Chateauneuf-du-Pape cannot satisfy. Christ came so that we may have life, and may have it more abundantly (John 10:10). Only through him can we discover true peace. Then we can say with the psalmist, "My cup runneth over" (Psalm 23:5)— spilling recklessly, lovingly, into the lives of others.

ENDNOTES

[1] Robert C. Fuller, *Religion and Wine: A Cultural History of Wine Drinking in the United States* (Knoxville: Univ. of Tennessee Press, 1996) Foreword by Jerald C. Brauer, vii.

[2] Ibid., vii-viii.

[3] Kurt Senske, *The Calling: Live a Life of Significance* (St Louis: Concordia Publishing House, 2011); Kurt Senske, *Personal Values: God's Game Plan for Life* (Minneapolis: Augsburg Books, 2004); Kurt Senske, *Executive Values: A Christian Approach to Organizational Leadership* (Minneapolis: Augsburg Books, 2003).

[4] Martin Luther, *Luther's Works*, ed. Hilton C. Oswald (St. Louis: Concordia Publishing House, 1995), 11:434.

[5] Letter to Abbe Morellet, http://en.wikiquote.org/wiki/Benjamin_Franklin#Sourced.

[6] Michael Kimmelman, *The Accidental Masterpiece: On the Art of Life and Vice Versa* (New York: Penguin Books, 2005), 5.

[7] Arthur W. Klinck, *Home Life in Bible Times* (St. Louis: Concordia Publishing House, 1969) 51-52.

[8] Paul L. Maier, *In The Fullness of Time: A Historian Looks At Christmas, Easter, and the Early Church* (Grand Rapids: Kregel, 1991), 127.

[9] Karen MacNeil, *The Wine Bible* (New York: Workman,

2001), 4.

[10] Quoted in Jay McInerney, *A Hedonist in the Cellar: Adventures in Wine* (New York: Alfred A. Knopf, 2006) xv-xvi.

[11] Ibid., xviii.

[12] Ibid., 163.

[13] Hugh Johnson, *A Life Uncorked* (Berkeley: Univ. of California Press, 2005), 62-63.

[14] MacNeil, *The Wine Bible*, 4.

[15] Johnson, *A Life Uncorked*, 15-16.

[16] Ibid., 49.

[17] Thomas Addington and Stephen Graves, "Balance: Life's Juggling Act," *Life@Work* (November-December 2000), 40,43, quoted in Senske, *Executive Values*, 149.

[18] MacNeil, *The Wine Bible*, 5.

[19] Kermit Lynch, *Adventures on the Wine Route* (New York: North Point Press, 1988), 23.

[20] Dietrich Bonhoeffer, *Discipleship* (Minneapolis: Fortress Press, 2001), 61-62.

[21] MacNeil, *The Wine Bible*, 5-6.

[22] Jay McInerney, *A Hedonist in the Cellar*, xviii.

[23] Edita Lausanne, ed., *Le Grand Livre Du Vin* (New York: World Publishing Co., 1970), 45.

[24] William K. McElvaney, "If God is to be real to us, we must do God's work," *Dallas Morning News*, December

30, 1995, 4G.

[25] MacNeil, *The Wine Bible*, 6.

[26] Johnson, *A Life Uncorked*, 261.

[27] MacNeil, *The Wine Bible*, 460.

[28] Maier, *In The Fullness of Time*, 17.

[29] Dietrich Bonhoeffer, *Letters and Papers from Prison*, ed. Ederhard Bethage (New York: Macmillan, 1953), 47-48.

[30] Edward Hyams, *Dionysus: A Societal History of the Wine Vine* (New York: Macmillan, 1965), 63.

[31] Morton T. Kelsey, "The Cross and the Cellar," in *Bread and Wine: Readings for Lent and Easter* (Maryknoll, NY: Orbis Books, 2003), 206, 210-211.

[32] Bonhoeffer, *Letters And Papers from Prison*, 23.

[33] John W. Matthews, "Bonhoeffer at 100," *The Lutheran*, (February 2006), 12-14.

[34] Johnson, *A Life Uncorked*, 153.

[35] MacNeil, *The Wine Bible*, 410.

[36] Lausanne, ed., *Le Grand Livre Du Vin*, 44.

[37] Johnson, *A Life Uncorked*, 261.

[38] Ibid., 187.

[39] MacNeil, *The Wine Bible*, 359.

[40] Mike Weiss, *A Very Good Year: The Journey of a California Wine from Vine to Table* (New York: Gotham Books, 2005), 188.

[41] Ibid., 36.

[42] Ibid., 163.

[43] Nancy Gibbs, "The Magic of the Family Meal," *Time* (June 12, 2006), 51-52.

[44] Ibid., 52.

[45] MacNeil, *The Wine Bible*, 82.

[46] Ibid., 16.

[47] Lynch, *Adventures on the Wine Route*, 47.

[48] Arthur Simon, *How Much is Enough? Hungering for God in an Affluent Culture* (Grand Rapids, MI: Basic Books, 2003), 54.

[49] Johnson, *A Life Uncorked*, 63.

[50] Joel Stein, "I Love Wine Camp," *Time* (October 16, 2006), 88.

[51] Ornella D'Allessio and Marco Santini, *Wine Country Europe: Touring, Tasting, and Buying in the Most Beautiful Wine Regions* (New York: Rizzoli, 2005), 106.

[52] Ibid., 109, 113.

[53] Lausanne, ed., *Le Grand Livre Du Vin*, 44.

[54] Eric Asimov, "Wine's Pleasures: Are They All In Your Head?" *The New York Times*, May 7, 2008, D1, D4.

[55] Johann Wolfgang von Goethe, *Faust*, lines 682-683, trans. Jaroslav Pelikan, www.stolaf.edu/news/speeches/pelikan.html.

[56] Richard Hays, *The Moral Vision of the New Testament: A Contemporary Introduction to New Testament Ethics* (San Francisco: Harper, 1996), 464-470.

[57] Ibid., 467.

[58] Mihaly Csikszentmihalyi, *Flow: The Psychology of Optimal Experience* (New York: Harper Perennial, 1991), 19.

[59] Barbara Cawthorne Crafton, "Living Lent," *Bread and Wine: Readings for Lent and Easter* (Maryknoll, NY: Orbis, 2005), 15, 18.

[60] Lynch, *Adventures on the Wine Route*, 114.

[61] Andre Vedel, ed., *The Hachette Guide to French Wines* (New York: Alfred Knopf, 1986), 14.

[62] Tom Harpur, *The Spirituality of Wine* (Kelowna, British Columbia: Northstone Publishing, 2004), 106.

[63] Lausanne, ed., *Le Grand Livre Du Vin*, 44.

[64] Amy Reiley, "The Health Benefits of Wine: Weighing the Pros and Cons," www.gayot.com/wine/feature/health-benefits-of-wine.html.

[65] Ibid.

[66] Christine Ansbacher, "Claret Cure: Drink two glasses of red wine and call me in the morning," *Chief Executive* (January/February, 2007), 60-61.

[67] Reiley, "The Health Benefits of Wine."

[68] Harpur, *The Spirituality of Wine*, 104.

[69] Reiley, "The Health Benefits of Wine."

[70] MacNeil, *The Wine Bible*, 161.

[71] Bradley Hanson, *A Graceful Life: Lutheran Spirituality for Today* (Minneapolis: Augsburg, 2000), 69.

[72] Matthew Harrison, "Though God Slay Me, I Will Yet Hope in Him," *Mercy Works* (Fall 2006/Winter 2007): 4, 7, fn.6.

[73] Vedel, ed., *The Hachette Guide to French Wines*, 11.

[74] Tom Harpur, *The Spirituality of Wine*, 36.

[75] MacNeil, *The Wine Bible*, 318.

[76] Gerald Asher, *The Pleasures of Wine* (San Francisco: Chronicle Books, 2002), 306.

[77] Maier, *In the Fullness of Time*, 125-128.

[78] Ibid., 127-128.

[79] See Matthew 27:33-34.

[80] MacNeil, *The Wine Bible*, 136-137.

[81] www.wrathofgrapes.com/winequot.html.

ABOUT THE AUTHOR

Dr. Kurt Senske serves as Chief Executive Officer of Lutheran Social Services of the South and has served as Chairman of Thrivent Financial, a Fortune 500 financial services organization. A gifted public speaker, Kurt has been a regular commentator on television and radio as well as a guest columnist for newspapers and magazines on a variety of issues. Kurt, his wife, Laurie, and their daughter, Sydney, live in Austin, Texas.

is certainly not a panacea, wine has an impressive number of beneficial qualities, many of which are noted in the Bible: it cheers God and man (Judges 9:13), gladdens the heart (Psalm 104:15), strengthens young men (2 Samuel 16:2), makes us merry (Esther 1:10; Ecclesiastes 10:19) and was given to those with heavy hearts or who were about to die (Proverbs 31:6).

The health-giving attributes of wine were documented early on by none other than Hippocrates, the father of medicine, who, around 400 B.C., observed, "Wine suits man marvelously well, if, in health as in illness, he uses it sensibly and in moderation, according to his individual constitution."[61] Other examples abound. An anonymous 13th-century poem from a wine lover's diary describes how wine "keepeth the stomach from wambling, the heart from swelling, the hands from shivering, the sinews from shrinking, the veins from crumbling, the bones from aching and the marrow from soaking."[62] Pope Innocent VII in the 14th century wrote in a letter to his son:

> "This Beaune wine that you sent Us has a good and agreeable taste. It is quite pleasing to Our palate and constitution. We have made almost regular use of it as a curative during our recent illness. Therefore, We . . . request that you send Us more as soon as the possibility arises."[63]

Noted London physician Dr. Peter Shaw in his 1724 book, *Juice of the Grape*, proclaimed that wine is preferable to water. And in the mid-1800s, famed French chemist Louis Pasteur declared, "Wine is the most healthful and most hygienic of beverages."[64]

In the 1980s, the cultural link between the consumption of wine and cardiovascular health gained a firmer foothold when researchers identified a significant factor in resolving the conundrum known as the French paradox—the fact that the French people, while eating a diet high in saturated fats, had a low incidence of heart disease. Researchers established that wine negates the damaging impact of high-fat foods, thereby reducing coronary heart